Nuffield Primary Science
SCIENCE PROCESSES AND CONCEPT EXPLORATION

Ages
5-7

TEACHERS' GUIDE

PUBLISHED FOR THE NUFFIELD–CHELSEA CURRICULUM TRUST BY COLLINS EDUCATIONAL

Contents

Explanation of symbols in the margins

 Warning

 Good opportunities to develop and assess work related to Experimental and Investigative Science

 Notes which may be useful to the teacher

 Vocabulary work

 Opportunities for children to use information technology

 Equipment needed

 Reference to the pupils' books

CHAPTER 1

Planning

1.1 The SPACE approach to teaching and learning science

A primary class where the SPACE approach to science is being used may not at first seem different from any other class engaged in science activities; in either, children will be mentally and physically involved in exploring objects and events in the world around them. However, a closer look will reveal that both the children's activities and the teacher's role differ from those found in other approaches. The children are not following instructions given by others; they are not solving a problem set them by someone else. They are deeply involved in work which is based on their own ideas, and they have taken part in deciding how to do it.

The teacher has, of course, prepared carefully to reach the point where children try out their ideas. She or he will have started on the topic by giving children opportunities to explore from their own experience situations which embody important scientific ideas. The teacher will have ensured that the children have expressed their ideas about what they are exploring, using one or more of a range of approaches – from whole class discussion to talking with individual children, or asking children to write or draw – and will have explored the children's reasons for having those ideas.

With this information the teacher will have decided how to help the children to develop or revise their ideas. That may involve getting the children to use the ideas to make a prediction, then testing it by seeing if it works in practice; or the children may gather further evidence to discuss and think about. In particular, the teacher will note how 'scientific' children have been in their gathering and use of evidence; and should, by careful questioning, encourage greater rigour in the use of scientific process skills.

It is essential that it is the children who change their ideas as a result of what they find themselves, and that they are not merely accepting ideas which they are told are better.

By carefully exploring children's ideas, taking them seriously and choosing appropriate ways of helping the children to test them, the teacher can move children towards ideas which apply more widely and fit the evidence better – those which are, in short, more scientific.

You will find more information about the SPACE approach in the Nuffield Primary Science *Science Co-ordinators' handbook*.

1.2 Useful strategies

Finding out children's ideas

This guide points out many opportunities for finding out children's ideas. One way is simply by talking, but there are many others. We have found the following strategies effective. How you use them may depend on the area of science you are dealing with. In the teachers' guides you will find examples of these strategies, with suggestions as to where you might use them. More information about them is given in the *Science Co-ordinators' handbook*.

Talking and open questioning

Whole class discussions can be useful for sharing ideas, but they do not always give all children a chance to speak. It is often helpful if children are allowed to think of their own ideas first, perhaps working them out in drawings, and are then encouraged to share these with others – perhaps with just one other child, or with a larger group.

Annotated drawings

Asking children to draw their ideas can give a particularly clear insight into what they think. It also gives you a chance to discuss the children's ideas with them. Words conveying these ideas can then be added to the drawing, either by you or by the child, in the course of discussion to clarify what has been represented. Such work can be kept as a permanent record.

Sorting and classifying

This can be a useful way of helping children to clarify their ideas and to record their thinking. They could sort a collection of objects or pictures into groups.

Writing down ideas

When they have acquired some writing skill, this gives children the opportunity to express their own views. It will usually be in response to questions posed by you.

Log books and diaries

These can be used to record changes over a longer period of time. They need not necessarily be kept by individual children, but could be kept by a group or class as a whole. Children can jot down, as words or drawings, the changes they notice and something about what they think are the reasons for what they observe.

Helping children to develop their ideas

Letting children try out their own ideas

This will involve children in using some of the process skills of science: at first mainly observing, predicting, and communicating. Later, as children approach Key Stage 2, they will begin to make more use of measuring, hypothesizing, planning and carrying out fair tests, and interpreting results and findings.

As often as possible, children should see what happens when they put their ideas to test. They should be encouraged to observe and report carefully what happens and to give their ideas about why it happens.

Encouraging generalization from one context to another

In discussing a particular event, for example dissolving sugar in tea, consider whether the explanation proposed applies in another context, such as salt dissolving on a wet road. You or the children might suggest other contexts where the idea might be tried. This might be done by discussing the evidence for and against the explanation, or by gathering more evidence and testing the idea in the other context, depending on children's familiarity with the events being examined.

Discussing the words children use to describe their ideas

Children can be asked to be quite specific about the meaning of words they use, whether scientific or not. They can be prompted to think of alternative words which have almost the same meaning. They can be asked to think of examples of a word they are using, such as 'melt', so that you can decide when to introduce alternative or more precise words if necessary.

Extending the range of evidence

Some of the children's ideas may be consistent with their experience up to that time, but they could be challenged by extending the range of this experience. This applies particularly to things which are not easily observed, such as slow changes; or those which are normally hidden, such as the insides of objects. Books are useful in some cases.

Getting children to communicate their ideas

Expressing ideas in any way – through writing, drawing, modelling or, particularly, through discussion – involves thinking them through, and often rethinking and revising them. Discussion has a further advantage in that it is two-way and children can set others' ideas against their own. Just realizing that there are different ideas helps them to reconsider their own.

1.3 Charts to help children to develop their ideas

The charts on pages 22, 33 and 44 show how you can help children to develop their ideas from starting points which have given rise to different ideas.

The centre rectangles contain starter questions.
The surrounding 'thought bubbles' contain the sort of ideas expressed by children.
The further ring of rectangles contains questions posed by teachers in response to the ideas expressed by the children. These questions are meant to prompt children to think about their ideas.
The outer rounded boxes indicate ways in which the children might respond to the teacher's questions.
Some of the shapes have been left blank, as a sign that other ideas may be encountered and other ways of helping children to develop their ideas may be tried.

1

This teachers' guide is divided into themes; in each one there is a section on finding out children's ideas, examples of ideas children have, and a section on helping children to develop their ideas.

1.4 Living things in their environment and the curriculum

Habitats

The aim of this theme is to help children understand that living things are suited to the places in which they live.

Most children will be aware that animals and plants live in different places. They might suggest that a place provides safety, food or warmth for animals and plants. Few are likely to mention that different habitats provide different conditions.

Children could visit different habitats such as a school field or hedgerow, observing how the habitat and the animals and plants within it change over a period of time. Visits to a zoo or farm could enable them to consider the needs of a broader range of animals. Children can draw, photograph and discuss their experiences. This will provide a basis for developing an understanding of the ways in which living things interact with their environment.

Life Processes and Living Things

3 Green plants as organisms
a that plants need light and water to grow.

5 Living things in their environment
a that there are different kinds of plants and animals in the local environment;
b that there are differences between local environments and that these affect which animals and plants are found there.

Understanding Living Things and the Processes of Life (Stages P1 to P3)

Interaction of living things with their environment
• animals and plants in a variety of habitats, to demonstrate variety and to show how living things depend on each other.

Waste and decay

This theme aims to familiarize children with the ways in which everyday waste changes over a period of time.

Young children often explain that waste materials will stay the same or that they will be moved by person, animal or the wind. Some children might mention that items will change colour or go rusty. A few may explain that some waste will rot.

Children can be helped to understand that some waste products decay naturally while others can be recycled or re-used. Children can record waste at home or at school, investigating changes in waste as well as considering some of the ways waste materials are reused in the classroom. Through discussion, visits and secondary sources, children will increase their awareness of what happens to household waste.

Effects of human activity on the environment

The ways in which humans affect their environment are explored in this theme.

Young children mention some of the negative ways people affect the places they inhabit such as dropping litter and breaking windows. Children can consider both the good and bad ways that people affect the places where they live. Observing the school and the surrounding area, talking to parents and grandparents as well as looking at secondary sources, should help children understand the variety of ways in which the place where they live has been affected by people.

This theme introduces children to micro-organisms, which are studied in Key Stage 2 (Sc2:5e).

This theme is now studied in the Geography National Curriculum at Key Stage 1.

Understanding Living Things and the Processes of Life (Stages P1 to P3)

Interaction of living things with their environment
• caring for living things in the classroom and the home.

1.5 Experimental and Investigative Science

Two important aspects of children's learning in science are:

◆ learning how to investigate the world around them;
◆ learning to make sense of the world around them using scientific ideas.

These are reflected in the National Curriculum. 'Experimental and Investigative Science' covers the first aspect. The second aspect is covered by the rest of the Programme of Study. Although these two aspects of science learning are separated in the National Curriculum they cannot be separated in practice and it is not useful to try to do so. Through investigation children explore their ideas and/or test out the ideas which arise from discussion. As a result, ideas may be advanced, but this will depend on the children's investigation skills. Thus it is important to develop these skills in the context of activities which extend ideas. So there is no separate Nuffield Primary Science teachers' guide on scientific investigations, because opportunities to make these occur throughout all the guides and they form an essential part of the SPACE approach.

AT 1 Thus in this guide you will find investigations which provide opportunities to develop and assess the skills and understanding set out in Experimental and Investigative Science. These are marked in the text by the symbol shown here. In this teachers' guide, the investigations which cover the most skills are 'Observing habitats' (page 23) and 'Investigating rust' (page 36).

It is important that teachers give active guidance to pupils during investigations to help them work out how to improve the way in which they plan and carry out their investigations.

Experimental and Investigative Science is about the ways scientific evidence can be obtained, about the ways observations and measurements are made, and about the way in which the evidence is analysed. It therefore sets out three main ways in which pupils can develop their ability to do experimental and investigative science, as follows:-

1 'Planning experimental work'. Here, children should be helped to make progress from asking general and vague questions, to suggesting ideas which could be tested. Teachers' discussion with pupils should aim to help them to make predictions, using their existing understanding, on the basis of which they can decide what evidence should be collected. This should lead them to think about what apparatus and equipment they should use.

When children describe plans for their work, they should be helped to think about what features they are going to change, what effects of these changes they are going to observe or measure, and what features they must keep the same. In this way they can come to understand what is meant by 'a fair test'.

2   'Obtaining evidence'. Children should make observations in the light of their ideas about what they are looking for and why. When they describe their observations, teachers may have to help them to improve, for example by reminding them of their original aims and plan for the work. Such help should also encourage progress from qualitative comparisons and judgements to appreciating the value of making quantitative measurements (for example 'cold water' is qualitative, 'water at 12°C' is quantitative). This should lead to the development of skills with a variety of instruments and to increasing care and accuracy in measurement, involving, for example, repeating measurements to check.

3   'Considering evidence'. Here, children should first learn to record their evidence in systematic and clear ways, starting with simple drawings and then learning to use tables, bar charts and line graphs to display the patterns in numerical data. Then they should be asked to think about and discuss their results, considering what might be learnt from any trends or patterns. As ideas develop, they should be careful in checking their evidence against the original idea underlying the investigation and should become increasingly critical in discussing alternative explanations which might fit their evidence. In such discussions, they should be helped to relate their arguments to their developing scientific understanding. They should also be guided to see possibilities for conducting their investigation more carefully, or in quite different ways.

Whilst these three may seem to form a natural sequence of stages, children's work might not follow this particular sequence. For example, some might start with evidence from their observations and proceed on this basis to propose a hypothesis and a plan to test it. For others, the results of one task may be the starting point for a new inquiry involving new measurements. Useful learning about how to investigate might arise when only one or two of the above aspects of an investigation are involved, or when the teacher tells children about some aspects so that they can concentrate on others. However, there should be some occasions for all pupils when they carry out the whole process of investigation by themselves.

The assessment examples given in chapter 3 are analysed in relation to the level descriptions, which describe children's progress in relation to these three aspects: *planning experimental work*, *obtaining evidence* and *considering evidence*. Thus, these three provide a framework both for guiding children and for assessing their progress in experimental and investigative work.

1.6 Planning your science programme in school

The following pages give examples of how two schools have planned their science programme for the whole of Key Stage 1. Planning of this kind helps to provide continuity and progression in children's learning in science. The development of such whole school programmes is discussed more fully in the *Science Co-ordinators' Handbook*.

Each plan covers the requirements for the National Curriculum at Key Stage 1 and shows which themes in the Nuffield Primary Science Teachers' Guides have been used for planning the topic in detail by the classteacher.

Example 1

This primary school has recently grown from 1.5 form entry to 2 form entry and so have had to take account of varying class sizes and vertical grouping. Their programme is based on fixed year topics which provide progression through the programme of study but by using the SPACE approach staff feel they are able to cater for individual children.

Each topic is planned out, by year group, in terms of the concept to be explored and the key ideas to be focused on using the Teachers' Guides. Some topics run for one term whilst others are restricted to half a term. A minimum of five lessons are allowed for each half term. Individual teachers use the topic plan to develop their own short term planning responding to the ideas of the children in their class.

	AUTUMN TERM	SPRING TERM		SUMMER TERM	
RECEPTION	Individual variation	Sources and uses of electricity	Light and dark	Changing materials	
Nuffield Primary Science Teachers' Guide	The variety of life 2.2	Electricity and magnetism 2.1	Light 2.1, 2.2	Materials 2.2	
Programme of Study †	Sc2:4a	Sc4:1a	Sc4:3a, b	Sc3:2a, b; Sc4:2d	
YEAR 1	Pushes and pulls	Making and hearing sounds	The human body and keeping healthy	Local habitats	Plants and animal growth
Nuffield Primary Science Teachers' Guide	Forces and movement 2.1 Using energy 2.2	Sound and music 2	Living processes 2.2	Living things in their environment 2.1 Rocks, soil and weather 2.1 Earth in space 2.3	Living processes 2.3
Programme of Study †	Sc4:2a, b, c, d	Sc4:3c, d, e	Sc2:2a, b, c, d, e, f	Sc2:5a, b	Sc2:2e; 3a, b, c
YEAR 2	Properties of materials	Magnets	Electricity - simple circuits	Naming and grouping living things	
Nuffield Primary Science Teachers' Guide	Materials 2.1 Rocks, soil and weather 2.1	Electricity and magnetism 2.3	Electricity and magnetism 2.2	The variety of life 2.1	
Programme of Study †	Sc3:1a, b, c, d, e	Sc3:1b, c	Sc4:1a, b, c	Sc2:1a, b; 4b	

Example 2

Situated in a large conurbation this primary school is 2.5 form entry but the number of children entering fluctuates from year to year causing difficulties with class size. The Nursery is an integral part of the school and work is shared with the Reception classes. Therefore this pre-YR1 time is planned as a whole providing a wide range of experiences for the children so that they are 'working towards' the requirements of the programme of study.

The plan is set out by year group and the different elements of the Programme of Study, covering five topics per year with each one to be covered in approximately half a term. Each year group decides the order of their topics during the year. The provision of a 'spare' half term allows teachers some flexibility in their planning and, if they wish, to introduce other aspects of science not prescribed by the National Curriculum.

	AUTUMN TERM		SPRING TERM		SUMMER TERM	
RECEPTION	This is me	Our school	Plants and animals	Homes - using electricity	Toys	
Nuffield Primary Science Teachers' Guide	The variety of life 2.2	Living things in their environment 2.3	Living things in their environment 2.1; Living processes 2.3	Electricity and magnetism 2.1	Forces and movement 2.1	
Programme of Study (working toward) †	Sc2:2a, b, f; 4a	Sc2:1a, 3b, 5a; Sc3:2a	Sc2:1b, 3a, b, c, 4b, 5a, b	Sc4:1a, 3a, b	Sc4:2a, b, c	
YEAR 1	Ourselves	Growing things	Materials - clothes	Sounds/Night and day	Floating and sinking	
Nuffield Primary Science Teachers' Guide	Living processes 2.2; Variety of life 2.2	Living processes 2.3	Materials 2.1	Sound and music 2; The earth in space 2.1	Forces and movement 2.2	
Programme of Study †	Sc2:1b; 2a, b, e, f; 4a, b	Sc2:3a, b, c	Sc3:1a, b, c, d, e; 2a	Sc4:3c, d, e	Sc3:1a, c, e; Sc4:2a	
YEAR 2	Keeping healthy	Habitats	Materials - homes	Light and electricity	Moving things	
Nuffield Primary Science Teachers' Guide	Living processes 2.2	The variety of life 2.1; Living things in their environment 2.1; Rocks, soil and weather 2.1	Materials 2.1; 2.2	Electricity and magnetism 2.1, 2.2; Light 2.1; 2.2	Forces and movement 2.1; Using energy 2.2	
Programme of Study †	Sc2:1b; 2b, c, d	Sc2:4b; 5a, b	Sc3:1a, b, c, d, e; 2b	Sc4:1a, b, c; 3a, b	Sc4:2a, b, c, d	

† For the purposes of these charts the references to sections of the Programme of Study have been abbreviated as follows:
Sc2 = Life Processes and Living Things
Sc3 = Materials and their Properties
Sc4 = Physical Processes

1.7 Planning a topic

Here is a case study which may help you in planning a topic.

Case study: Shopping

The teacher was keen to put children's study of science into a topic on shopping. In this way children could use their everyday experiences to look at Living things in the environment. Within the topic there was scope for children of all abilities to develop their ideas about waste and the effects of human activity on the environment. Some links with English, Maths and Geography were planned.

The starting point for the topic was a visit to the busy local market. Children drew pictures of what they had noticed during that visit; they also recorded their ideas about what the area might have looked like before the market was established. Following their visit children drew pictures of what they thought would happen to some of the waste from the market. Groups of children were then encouraged to develop their ideas through investigation and by using secondary sources. Finally children shared their experiences with each other through discussion, posters, collages and models, and role play.

SCIENCE

Effects of human activity on the environment

- Using sequenced drawings children described what they noticed about the shopping area and what they thought it had looked like before.

- They considered the changes that had been made to the neighbourhood as a result of the shops, drawing pictures of roads, pavements, toilets, street lights, and bus stops.

- The selection of vegetables and fruits available led to a discussion of how production of these change the landscape.

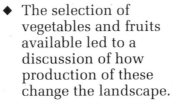

Waste

- Children drew pictures of the sorts of waste materials the shops would make; they recorded what might happen to the waste.

- They observed changes in a group of items over several weeks and recorded what they noticed in a class diary.

- Ideas about how and why some waste materials change were exchanged during investigations and discussion.

LINKS WITH OTHER CURRICULUM AREAS

English

◆ Children made a poster advertising the class shop.

◆ They wrote stories or sequenced pictures describing their visit to the shops.

◆ They wrote poems describing fruit they had noticed. (Looks like … tastes like …)

◆ A discussion of how people both improve and harm the place where they live formed the basis for a school assembly.

Mathematics

A shop was made in the classroom which enabled the children to use their understanding of money.

◆ Buying sweets and biscuits allowed children to develop their number skills.

◆ Some children counted the number of sweets and biscuits contained in a packet and were able to practise sharing these between different groups of friends.

◆ Other children sorted toffees and biscuits according to shape.

Geography

◆ Children matched pictures of goods to the shop where they were bought.

◆ They produced maps of their visits to the shops showing familiar landmarks.

◆ Pictures and photographs of different shopping areas were collected and children discussed why shops were situated near roads.

1.8 Pupils' books

The pupils' book accompanying this guide is called *A first look at where things live*. The pupils' books are intended to be used spread by spread. The spreads are not sequential, and they are covered in these notes in thematic order.

Features of the pupils' books include:
◆ Stimulus spreads, often visual, designed to raise questions, arouse curiosity, and to promote discussion.

◆ Information spreads, which give secondary source material in a clear and attractive way.

◆ Activity ideas, to form the basis of investigations to be carried out by the children.

◆ Cross-curricular spreads and stories which can act as a basis for creative writing, or spreads with a historical or creative focus.

◆ Real life examples of applications of science in the everyday world.

Where do they live? pages 2-3

Purpose: Information about animals which move in different ways, and the fact that some can move in more than one way, depending on their habitat.
Notes: The earthworm wriggles and burrows (underground). The mallard (duck) can swim, fly and walk. The bat can fly and hangs upside down to sleep; it can also eat while it flies. Cats can climb and walk. Snails slide on a trail of mucus.
Question for discussion: How do your pets at home move?
Teachers' guide cross references: *Living things in their environment*, pages 27-8; *Living processes*, page 11.

What lives in a garden? pages 4–5

Purpose: A discussion spread showing a familiar habitat with a variety of living things in it, to encourage children to identify living creatures in their own gardens or local parks.
Pupils' book cross-references: *A first look at different plants and animals*, pages 14-17, *A first look at light*, pages 4-5.
Teachers' guide cross-reference: *Living things in their environment*, page 23.

Elephants pages 8–9

Purpose: A reading spread to help children develop their ideas about extinction and the need for conservation.
Notes: The elephants are presented in their natural habitat, not a zoo. The spread raises awareness about a specific conservation issue (the need to stop killing elephants for ivory), but should provoke general discussion.
Pupils' book cross-reference: *A first look at different plants and animals*, pages 14-15.
Teachers' guide cross-reference: *Living things in their environment*, page 25, 48.

Can I take these home, Miss? pages 20-21

Purpose: A reading spread about a less familiar (seaside) habitat to introduce children to the idea that some living things can only live in one habitat, and to discourage them from taking things from their natural environments.
Question for discussion: Why should we leave things in their natural habitats?
Teachers' guide cross-references: *Living things in their environment*, pages 24-25, 48.

Look at those feet! pages 10-11

Purpose: To introduce children to the idea of adaptation through a matching game.
Notes: The matches are: mallard ducks – webbed feet with brown feathers; thrush – perching feet on branch; owl – claws; gannet – webbed feet with white feathers.
Questions for discussion: What are the birds' feet for? (The owl, for example, has four claws, two facing backwards, two forwards, for grabbing and holding prey.) What do you think your own feet are for? How are they adapted to where you live?
Teachers' guide cross-reference: *Living things in their environment*, page 28.

Hiding pages 14-15

Purpose: To introduce children to the idea of camouflage (more adaptation).
Notes: There are 26 frogs in the picture. The animals photographed are a deer, which uses colour for camouflage, a toad, which uses texture and colour and a polar bear, which uses colour. The animals also keep still in order to make them hard to see.
Pupils' book cross-references: *A first look at light*, pages 4-5.
Teachers' guide cross-references: *Living things in their environment*, pages 24-5.

The animals' picnic pages 16–17

Purpose: To introduce children, by way of a story, to the idea that animals eat different things and are adapted for particular diets.
Extension activity: Talk about why the animals left the picnic.
Teachers' guide cross-reference: *Living things in their environment*, page 24.

The litter bin game pages 6–7

Purpose: A 'fun' spread to start children thinking about the idea of decay and the need to dispose of rubbish carefully.
Notes: The game is played in pairs. Players need six counters each and a dice between them. Shake the appropriate number to 'put' the rubbish in the bin.
Teachers' guide cross-references: *Living things in their environment*, pages 34-5.

One green apple pages 12-13

Purpose: A starting point for a consideration of the idea of natural decay.
Extension activities: Run a controlled experiment in which an apple is put into an almost airtight container (it must not be fully airtight) and the stages in decay are observed and recorded by the children. Alternatively, you could leave an apple out of doors.
Teachers' guide cross-reference: *Living things in their environment*, page 37.

Containers pages 18-19

Purpose: To introduce children to the idea of recycling rubbish.
Notes: Children should identify the containers in the picture and think what they are made of. Ask, what happens to their own rubbish and what is done with it after it is taken away by the bin men?
Extension activities: Locate bottle banks and recycling facilities in the area of the school. Set up a recycling plant in the school for charity. Set a technology task to make something discarded into something useful. For example, a washing-up liquid container can be made into a pencil-holder.
Teachers' guide cross-references: *Living things in their environment*, pages 10, 34.

How Peter saved his town pages 22-23

Purpose: A story to introduce children to the idea that natural environments can be changed and habitats created by people: here by building dykes.
Extension activity: Relate this spread to the story of Hendrika from *The cow who fell in the canal* by Phyllis Krasilovsky (Little Mammoth/ Octopus Books).
Pupils' book cross-reference: A first look at moving things, pages 10-11.
Teachers' guide cross-references: *Living things in their environment*, page 48-9; *Rocks, soil and weather*, page 39.

1.9 Resources

This is what you may need to carry out the investigations shown in this book.

Access to the school grounds, and other areas of the local environment which are safely accessible
Classroom pets (in accordance with LEA and RSPCA guidelines)
Modelling clay or Plasticine
Magnifying glass
Pictures of roads, fields, cars, houses, toilets
A selection of clean waste materials:
    plastic bottles
    crisp packets
    egg boxes
    sweet wrappers
    various metal objects
    vegetables and fruits
Pictures of plants and animals, and ways in which humans have affected the local environment

1.10 Warnings

Activities which need particular care are indicated by this symbol in the margin. Everything possible should be done to ensure the safety of the children during their investigations. You should consult any guidelines produced by your own Local Education Authority and, if your school or LEA is a member, by CLEAPSS. See also the Association for Science Education publication *Be safe! some aspects of safety in school science and technology for Key Stages 1 and 2* (2nd edition, 1990). This contains more detailed advice than can be included here.

The points listed below require particular attention.

Take care when handling litter and other forms of rubbish – protect hands with disposable gloves or plastic bags.
Consider immunization against tetanus for both teachers and children.
Mouldy material produces spores to which some people are allergic. All mouldy material should be kept in sealed containers which are not opened. Avoid glass containers.
Children should wash their hands thoroughly after handling any rubbish or similar materials.
Fieldwork and visits must be carefully organized and supervised. Beware of dog mess and poisonous plants. Check your school's policy on visits.

AREAS FOR INVESTIGATION

◆ Exploring different habitats.

◆ Observing short and long term changes in a particular habitat.

◆ Examining the conditions needed for plants and animals to live.

◆ Investigating ways of caring for various animals and plants.

KEY IDEAS

◆ Living things live in a variety of places which are called habitats.

◆ Living things are suited to the places in which they live.

◆ Living things need certain conditions to stay alive.

◆ *Living things respond to changes in their environment.

◆ *Plants are the ultimate source of food for all living things.

◆ *Living things interact with each other in various ways, including competition for resources.

(*Asterisks indicate ideas which will be developed more fully in later key stages.)

A LOOK AT where things live

The places where living things live are called habitats. Each habitat provides conditions such as shelter, warmth, moisture, oxygen and food. Each habitat has its own particular set of conditions.

Animals and plants have certain features which suit them to a particular habitat: the animals and plants found in the local pond will differ from those living in the park.

Living things respond to changes in their habitat. Animals may leave a habitat if their food supply is threatened. Some plants need more sunlight than others, and will not survive if the habitat becomes shaded.

Food is the source of energy which all living things need to live. Plants are the ultimate source of food. Animals may feed directly on plants or they may eat other animals; the food of these other animals will ultimately have been provided by plants.

Finding out children's ideas
■ STARTER ACTIVITIES

! Check the area so that things like dog mess, broken glass, and poisonous plants can be avoided

Where do animals and plants live?

A class discussion can be used to stimulate children's ideas about the kinds of places in which animals and plants might live. You could have this discussion following a visit to an actual habitat, preferably in the school grounds.

Q *What sorts of places do animals and plants live in?*
What kinds of animals and plants might you find there?
Why do you think that is a good place for the animals and plants you have mentioned?

Q *Can you draw an animal/plant in the place where it might live?*
Why do you think the animal/plant lives here?
Could it live anywhere else?

Some children may be able to add to their drawings or discuss the things that animals/plants need to live.

Q *What do you think the animal/plant needs to live?*
How does it get what it needs?

Find out if the children are aware that other animals/plants might live in the same place or in different surroundings.

Q *Are there any other animals/plants that might be able to live here?*
Can you name other places where you might find different animals/plants?

Children's ideas

Where animals and plants live

Children suggest a range of places where animals live.

Many children explain that animals live in a particular place because they like it in that place.

> *It's dark, the worm likes it dark.*

A few children believe that the place should be safe. They might mention that the place needs to provide some protection from people or other animals.

> *Worms eat dead plants. Darkness so no-one can trample them.*

Children might mention the food animals need. Some drawings reveal an awareness that food should be available in the habitat.

> *My snail needs water, mud and leaves.*

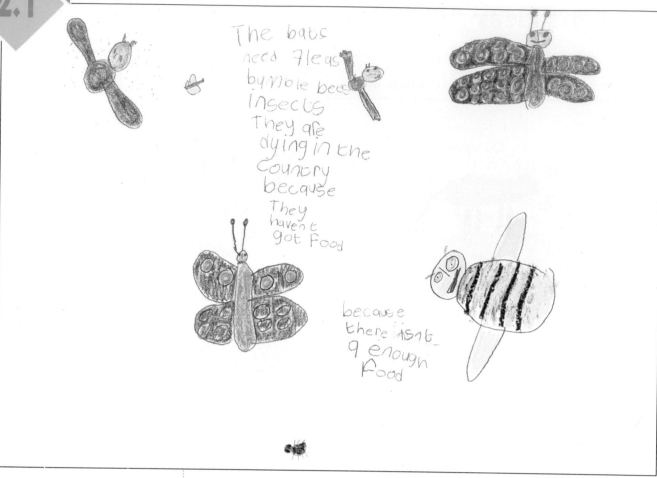

The bats need fleas bumble bee insects They are dying in the country because They haven't got food

because there isnt enough Food

This child describes how a shortage of food affects the number of bats in a habitat.

When asked about plants, young children tend to suggest a limited range of places where plants can live, such as plant pots on a windowsill, or in the garden. A few children might draw a tree on some grass.

Some children mention that plants need care in order to live.

> *They need you to keep an eye on them because they might die.*

Most children mention some of the things a plant might need to live, such as water, sun and soil. The water may be provided by a person, or by rain.

Children rarely describe how the sun, soil or water help the plant to live. Generally, children explain that the plants get thirsty. A few children might be aware that the amount of water could affect the plant's health.

> It needs water outside in the garden. Every time it rains it gets water. Too much water kills it.

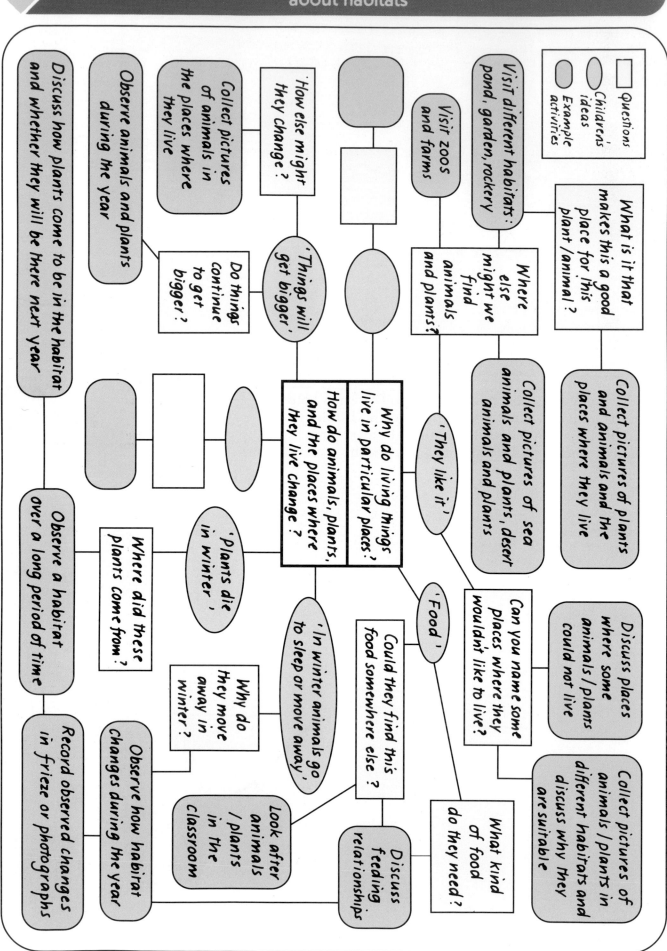

Key:

☐ Questions

⬭ Children's ideas

⬬ Example activities

Visit different habitats: pond, garden, rockery

Visit zoos and farms

What is it that makes this a good place for this plant/animal?

Where else might we find animals and plants?

Collect pictures of plants and animals and the places where they live

How else might they change?

'Things will get bigger'

Do things continue to get bigger?

Collect pictures of animals in the places where they live

Observe animals and plants during the year

Discuss how plants come to be in the habitat and whether they will be there next year

Collect pictures of sea animals and plants, desert animals and plants

'They like it'

Why do living things live in particular places?

How do animals, plants, and the places where they live change?

Collect pictures of animals/plants in different habitats and discuss why they are suitable

Discuss places where some animals/plants could not live

Can you name some places where they wouldn't like to live?

'Plants die in winter'

Where did these plants come from?

'Food'

Could they find this food somewhere else?

'In winter animals go to sleep or move away'

Why do they move away in winter?

Look after animals/plants in the classroom

Discuss feeding relationships

What kind of food do they need?

Observe a habitat over a long period of time

Observe how habitat changes during the year

Record observed changes in frieze or photographs

Helping children to develop their ideas

The chart opposite shows how you can help children to develop their ideas from starting points which have given rise to different ideas.

1 Observing habitats

Children should visit two habitats, one of which they may have looked at in the starter activity.

Teachers have successfully used parts of the school field, nearby wasteland, a hedge, a school garden, and even the school wall for habitat studies. Choose something which is safe and easily accessible.

Daily as well as long term changes may be observed. The study could take place over a few weeks or at intervals during the year.

Children will need to return to the area at different times during the study, so they should think about how they will find the exact place again. A good way is to mark out a patch about 1 metre square with string stretched between wooden stakes.

Children can take photographs of the area so that these, together with drawings and writing, provide a record of the first visit. They could record what they see on each visit on a frieze.

! Investigative work with living things has ethical and legal obligations, so choose practical investigations with care. The collection of plants and animals from the wild is severely restricted – see 'Animals and plants in schools: legal aspects' (DES Administrative memorandum 3/90)

t A small area which shows noticeable change will encourage children to observe closely

! Follow school or LEA rules about supervision. Check your school's policy on visits

! Take care that people do not fall over the string

! Be especially careful about ponds. (See 'Safety and the school pond' in *Primary science review,* Summer 1988.)

Q *What do you notice about the habitat?*
Do a lot of people come near the habitat, or is it undisturbed?
Is it wet or dry?
Is it warm or cold?
Is it sunny or shaded?
Is it windy or sheltered?

Encourage the children to consider how the animals and plants might be suited to this place:

Q *What kind of animals do you notice?*
Where are the animals?
What are they doing?
Will the same animals be here the next time you visit?
What plants do you notice?
Why is this a good place for these plants?
What would the plants need to live here?

Encourage the children to observe different parts of the plants carefully.

Q *Do all the plants have flowers?*
Are all the plants the same size?
Are the plants still alive when they lose their flowers?
What will the plants be like the next time you visit?

Children should draw or photograph some of the animals and plants they notice. These should form the basis for class discussions.

Q *What are the animals and plants eating in the habitat?*
What makes this a good place for these animals and plants?
Could any other plants or animals live in this habitat?
How will the area have changed on your next visit?

2 Animals and plants in different habitats

Visiting different habitats such as a farm or a pond can help children to develop their ideas. Ask questions which will help children think about what the animals and plants need to live.

Q *Where did you notice the [ducks]?*
What were they doing?
What food does the [duck] eat?
What did they look like?
Why do you think they have [feet] like that?
What other animals did you notice at the [pond]?
What would they need to live?
What kind of plants did you notice at the [pond]?
Were the flowers in a shaded or sunny spot?
Was the area wet or dry?

Encourage children to notice whether the plants are at different stages of their life cycle.

Q *How do you think the plants came to be there?*
Are they all flowering?
What are the flowers for?
In what ways might the plant change?
Will the plants grow again in the same place next year?

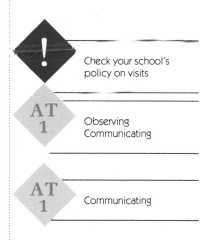

2.1

! Warn children about poisonous plants – especially attractive fruits and berries. Teach them never to taste any part of a plant unless a grown-up says that it is safe

Zoos can provide children with some experience of different habitats. Ask children to consider the needs of various animals, and how their needs might differ.

Q *What does the monkey need to live?*
What do the snakes need to live?
What were the animals doing?
What were they eating?
What would happen at the zoo if the fish lived in the same place as the sealions?

Some children will have had difficulty noticing some animals. Use these difficulties to talk about the value of camouflage.

Q *Why could you not see the lizard on the stone?*
Why would it be useful for the animal to be able to hide?

A first look at where things live has some camouflage pictures. Secondary sources, such as videos and books, can provide more information about how animals live in their natural habitats.

Let children make their own zoo in school, with model animals. Ask questions that will encourage them to use their knowledge of the range of things which animals need to live.

Q *What kind of place does the giraffe need to live?*
Which animals can you put together?
Which animals would need to be in different places?

! Check your school's policy on visits

 AT 1 Observing Communicating

 AT 1 Communicating

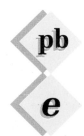 **pb**

e

AT
1

Observing
Communicating

3 Caring for animals in the classroom

Children could bring pictures of their own pets into school, so that the whole class can become familiar with the needs of a wider group of animals. Encourage close observation of a classroom pet.

Q *What sort of food does the [rabbit] eat?*
How does it manage to pick up the food?
What does the fish use to swim about?
What does the [stick insect] need to live?

A first look at living things gives examples of animals that might be kept as pets. Children can use these for the basis of a discussion about caring for pets.

Let each child make a poster or a book about one of the animals, describing the place where the animal lives as well as the things it needs to live.

4 Plants in the classroom

Let children take care of some plants in school. Ask questions to help children notice that the plants have different needs.

Q *Where do you find the plants in school?*
Do all the plants live on windowsills?
Do all the plants need watering every day?

5 Animal collage

Children can build up a collage of pictures of different animals showing some of the places where they might live. A class discussion will encourage children to think about the needs of some of the animals.

Q *Where would you find these animals?*
Would you find any of them in the same place?
What do these animals need to live?

Encourage children to consider which features suit the animal to its habitat.

Q *Why does the [pelican] have [a large beak]?*

Further questions could encourage children to think about what animals feed on.

Q *What kinds of food might the penguins eat?*
What would happen if the spider and the fly were together?

A first look at where things live gives examples of animals that live in different places. These can be used for information and the basis for further discussion.

pb

6 Plant collage

Children could make a collage of plant pictures including places where the plants live. A class discussion will familiarize children with the needs of a range of plants.

Q *Where would you find this ivy/cactus/lily?*
What would it need to live?

Plants have particular requirements

A first look at different plants and animals encourages children to think about the habitats in which different plants might be found. This could provide the basis for discussions.

pb

Plants and where they live

pb

7 Matching animals and plants to the places they live within a habitat

Give children pictures of different animals and plants and the places they might live within a habitat. You could use the ones in *A first look at where things live.*

Q *Can you match the animals and plants with the places where they would live?*

Group or class discussions could help children think about why animals and plants are suited to where they live.

8 What is this animal's name and where should it live?

Living things have features which are helpful to them

This game can extend children's knowledge of the needs of different animals and plants. Give children a series of clues about an animal or a plant until they are able to guess the plant or animal and suggest where it could live.

Q *This animal is covered in fur.*
The animal eats fish.
It lives in cold places.
The animal can swim in water.

pb

A first look at where things live shows how different kinds of bird have different kinds of feet. Children can use this material as the basis for discussion about how animals are adapted to habitats and ways of food gathering.

2.2 Waste and decay

A LOOK AT
waste and decay

◆ Examining the range of waste materials produced by human activities.

◆ Examining how various everyday waste products might change.

◆ Recording changes in waste products.

KEY IDEAS

◆ Some materials change and decay quickly, while for others the changes only occur over a long time.

◆ *Many human activities produce waste materials which can cause changes to occur in the environment, locally and/or globally.

◆ *Materials can be re-used, recycled or discarded.

(*Asterisks indicate ideas which will be developed more fully in later key stages.)

People throughout the world produce a variety of waste materials. Most waste from British homes is taken away by refuse collectors. Certain waste, such as vegetable peelings, will decay in suitable conditions (for instance a compost heap); the material will soften and break up. Other waste material is usually dumped at a landfill site, such as a disused gravel pit. When the site is full it is covered with earth, and some attempt may be made to landscape it.

Some waste will not rot. This may also be dumped, on land or at sea. Sometimes it is burnt.

Not all waste needs to be thrown away. A few things such as milk bottles can be re-used as they are. Other glass, and paper, metal and to a certain extent plastics, can be recycled and made into new items. The proportion of British rubbish that is recycled is still very small, but growing.

Rubbish may be contaminated. It should be enclosed so that it cannot be handled.
Fermentation may cause gas pressure to rise.
Wear gloves when collecting waste or litter.
Protect children from sharp pieces of metal.
Do not allow children to handle glass.
Some people are allergic to mould spores

Finding out children's ideas
■ STARTER ACTIVITIES

What happens to household rubbish?

To reveal children's ideas about how household rubbish might change, you could ask them to list the things that are thrown away at home or give them a selection of (clean) rubbish to look at. Encourage them to think about what will happen to these things.

Q *What kinds of things do you think are used up and thrown away during the day?*
Can you draw the rubbish as it is now, and how it will look in two weeks?
Can you sort the rubbish into things that will look the same and things that might change?

Choose one of the items from a child's list or pile of rubbish, and ask:

Q *What will happen to it?*
If we leave it in the bin will it stay the same or will it change?

Children's ideas

What happens to household rubbish?

Some children have little awareness of what happens to the rubbish after it has been placed in the dustbin. Most children just say that the binmen take it away. Some may mention that it goes to a central collection area such as a scrapyard.

There is little awareness that some rubbish is sorted. Most young children seem to believe that all the rubbish is treated in the same way. Some children suggest that rubbish is burnt after it has been collected.

this is the bin men cuming to or door and he is geting the bin bag and he is going to the scrap yard

> *I threw a bean tin away. It went in a big tip with the sausages. The tip went on a big wagon and was taken far away to the woods and put on a big fire. Then the fire went out and there was loads of dirty black mess.*

Occasionally, children mention that rubbish could be re-used, but usually they do not distinguish between re-used in its original form and recycled.

The bin wagin is takeing bin bags to the fatre the food gets braed agin so we can have food agin.

31

2.2

Children typically believe that changes to waste materials are brought about by human intervention.

> *A girl stood on the orange peel and it would go squashy.*
>
> *Wood would stay on the ground until the bin men came.*

Children may be aware of changes brought about by weather. They often mention that objects would become dirty or wet, or would be blown away by the wind. Some children may decide that items will change by rusting. Young children rarely suggest that items would rot. Occasionally, they mention the colour changes they notice in items such as apple cores.

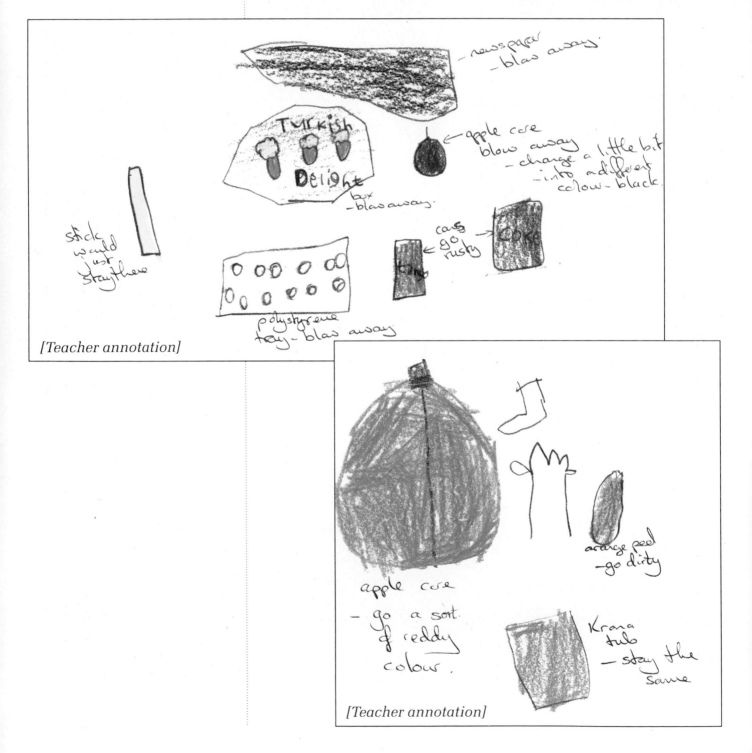

[Teacher annotation]

[Teacher annotation]

32

Helping children to develop their ideas about waste and decay

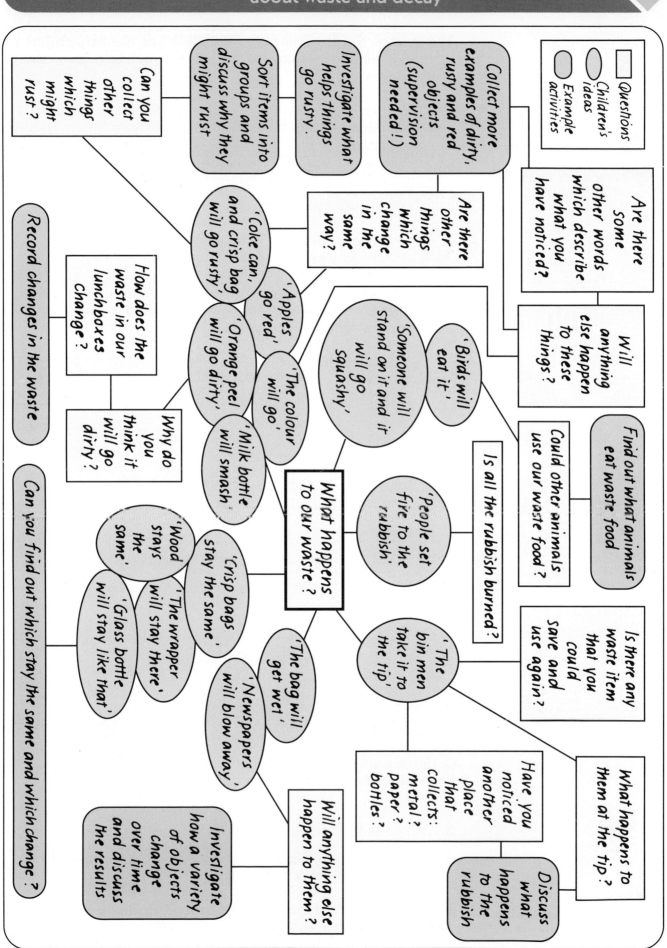

Key:
- Questions
- Children's ideas
- Example activities

Collect more examples of dirty, rusty and red objects (supervision needed!)

Investigate what helps things go rusty.

Sort items into groups and discuss why they might rust

Can you collect other things which might rust?

Are there some other words which describe what you have noticed?

Will anything else happen to these things?

Are there other things which change in the same way?

'Coke can, and crisp bag will go rusty'

'Apples go red'

'Orange peel will go dirty'

'The colour will go'

'Milk bottle will smash'

'Someone will stand on it and it will go squashy'

'Birds will eat it'

How does the waste in our lunchboxes change?

Record changes in the waste

Why do you think it will go dirty?

'Wood stays the same'

'The wrapper will stay there'

'Crisp bags stay the same'

'Glass bottle will stay like that'

'Newspapers will blow away'

'The bag will get wet'

What happens to our waste?

'People set fire to the rubbish'

'The bin men take it to the tip'

Is all the rubbish burned?

Could other animals use our waste food?

Find out what animals eat waste food

Is there any waste item that you could save and use again?

What happens to them at the tip?

Have you noticed another place that collects: metal? paper? bottles?

Discuss what happens to the rubbish

Will anything else happen to them?

Investigate how a variety of objects change over time and discuss the results

Can you find out which stay the same and which change?

Helping children to develop their ideas

The chart on the previous page shows how you can help children to develop their ideas from starting points which have given rise to different ideas.

1 Household rubbish

To consider the range of waste products produced by different human activities, children could keep a diary of what is thrown away at home over a weekend. Discuss the variety of things that have been thrown away. Then ask:

Q *What happens to the water after you have had a bath? What happens to the rubbish that we throw away?*

A first look at where things live gives examples of some domestic waste that can be recycled. This could be used as the basis for further discussions.

Warn children not to handle rubbish, and about safety and hygiene

AT 1   Observing Communicating

pb

Children could interview a school cook or caretaker about what happens to waste materials and rubbish at school.

2 What is left in the lunchbox?

After lunch children might look at what is left in a lunchbox to investigate how rubbish might change.

Q *What kinds of things are left in your lunchbox after you have finished eating?*

t   Some waste changes with time

Will it stay the same?
What could we do with it to find out?
Can you draw what is in the lunchbox as it looks now, and as it might look in four weeks' time?

Children could investigate what happens to the rubbish from the lunchbox over a month.

 Where might you put the waste from the lunchbox?
Should you leave the waste where you can see it, so you can be sure to notice if it begins to change?

Each item should be placed in a transparent sealed container such as a plastic bag or old lemonade bottle (avoid glass) at the beginning of the test, and the whole thing disposed of unopened at the end.

 How will you remember what the things looked like?

Seal containers sufficiently tightly to trap spores, but not so tightly that gas from fermentation cannot escape. Avoid temperatures higher than about 20 °C (room temperature), in case the growth of bacteria which favour human body temperature (37 °C) is encouraged

Encourage the children to keep a record of what the rubbish looks like now, so they can identify any changes. They may decide to draw pictures of the waste or to photograph it.

A class diary will enable children to draw or write about changes they noticed during the investigation. Encourage children to discuss these changes.

AT 1 — Communicating

 What do you notice now about the things from the lunchbox?
Have all the things changed?
Can you sort the items into things that have changed and things that have stayed the same?
How have they changed?
Why do you think those things have changed?
What can you say about those things that didn't change?

! Children should view the waste but not handle it

AT 1 — Interpreting results and findings

35

3 Objects which rust

Children's beliefs about which objects rust may be developed by providing them with a wide range of objects, including things which are red or brown, tarnished items, coins, old cutlery, rusted and tarnished nails, old steel wool and old pieces of copper wire.

Q *Can you put together the things that could rust?*

During the group discussions encourage children to exchange ideas about rusting.

Q *What do you think rust might be?*
What made you say these things are rusty?
How do you know when something is rusty?
How does rust happen?
Where else have you noticed rust?

Discussion of other things which rust could help children to consider what is happening when objects rust.

Q *Where do you find rust on [your bike]?*
What do you think is happening to make the rust?
Where do you leave [your bike]?
Why do you think [your bike or the car] goes rusty?

4 Investigating rust

Help children to plan investigations which will enable them to develop their ideas about why some items rust. Children could investigate their hypotheses about why a bicycle goes rusty, using nails instead. They could put nails in warm, cold, light, dark, dry and wet places.

Q *How will you decide whether somewhere is warm or cold?*
Will you wet all the nails or keep one dry?
Will you wet the nail completely or put it half in water with the top half dry?
What about trying different metals?

Children could cover nails in different substances such as paint, grease, and polythene – supervise this carefully.

Give children an opportunity to discuss their results.

Q *How could you stop a bicycle from rusting?*

5   Waste in the garden

The school or local park gardener, or a parent might talk to the children about garden waste. The children might ask:

> *What kind of rubbish do you have to deal with?*
> *Where do you put it?*
> *Does it change if it is left lying about?*
> *How does it change?*
> *Is there any rubbish that you can use again?*
> *Why do you use garden waste again?*
> *How is it used?*

A first look at where things live encourages children to think about what happens to garden waste and could be used as a basis for further discussion.

The gardener might be able to show children a compost heap and talk about what kinds of waste material it consists of and whether it contains anything alive.

 t
Iron and steel rust (steel rusts faster); most other metals corrode less noticeably

AT 1   Communicating

 pb

! Safety and hygiene are essential here

! The teacher/gardener should wear gloves when showing the children what is in the compost heap

Raising questions will help children observe the compost heap more closely.

Q *What do you notice about the heap?*
What kinds of things are there in the heap?
Can you tell which things have been there a long time, and which things are new?
Is the compost heap wet or dry?
What do you think the compost will look like in two more weeks?

Children could measure the temperature of the compost heap using a thermometer (avoid glass ones). You could take the children back to the heap to monitor any changes that take place. The children could compare this compost with potting compost bought from a garden centre.

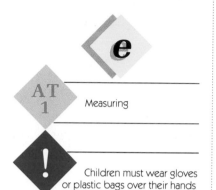

AT
1   Measuring

! Children must wear gloves or plastic bags over their hands if they handle compost/rubbish

Q *What do they look like?*
Do they look different?
Do they feel different?
Do they smell different?

6   Re-using materials

Children often bring discarded items into school to be re-used: old shirts are used as overalls, margarine tubs becomes plant pots, detergent bottles are made into models. A class discussion can help them to think about the way in which some of the materials they use can be re-used:

AT
1   Communicating

Q *What kinds of things do you use? Why?*
What happens to them?
Could some of them be used again?

Children should become aware that some items are re-used for their original purpose, while others are re-used in different ways.

A first look at where things live contains examples of domestic waste that are recycled, which could provide a starting point for discussion.

Q *Can you make a collection of items that are re-used in the same ways and another of those that are used in different ways?*

Suggest a few items to start them off – carrier bags, jam jars, newspapers – without saying which group they belong to.

Sequenced drawings that show how an item is used initially, and then how it is used again in school, could provide a record of the activity.

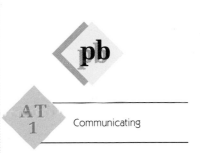

pb

AT 1 — Communicating

2.3 Effects of human activity on the environment

AREAS FOR INVESTIGATION

◆ Observing the local environment.

◆ Exploring how it might be improved.

KEY IDEA

◆ Human activity has changed all parts of the environment.

A LOOK AT the effects of human activity on the environment

The results of human activity are apparent in urban, rural and wild environments, locally and worldwide. The effects can be both good and bad:

◆ building houses improves people's living conditions, but also calls for mining and quarrying;

◆ roads are needed to enable people and materials to move from place to place, but vehicles use up limited resources of land and fuel and cause air pollution;

◆ improved drainage and sewerage systems in some countries have almost eliminated many diseases, but disposing of sewage into the sea contaminates it.

Finding out children's ideas

■ STARTER ACTIVITIES

How people affect their environment

Explore children's ideas about how people's actions affect the environment. Encourage them to consider the ways in which people improve the places where they live, as well as ways in which they may damage the environment.

Draw a large outline map of the area around the school and collect some pictures of things like broken windows, litter, cars, lorries, toilets, busy main roads, quiet residential roads, gardens, animals. Make these into cards and ask the children to place them on the picture to show different things done to their environment by people.

Q *If you walked around the town where do you think you might see some of these things?*

You might ask children to draw the place where they live, showing the kinds of things people do to it. They could prepare a 'radio broadcast'.

Q *What kinds of things around us have been done by people?*
What do you think makes this a nice place to live?
What do people do that makes it less nice?

Children's ideas

Most children suggest that litter is the main effect that humans have on the environment.

> *There will be rubbish all over the place.*
> *There is paper everywhere.*

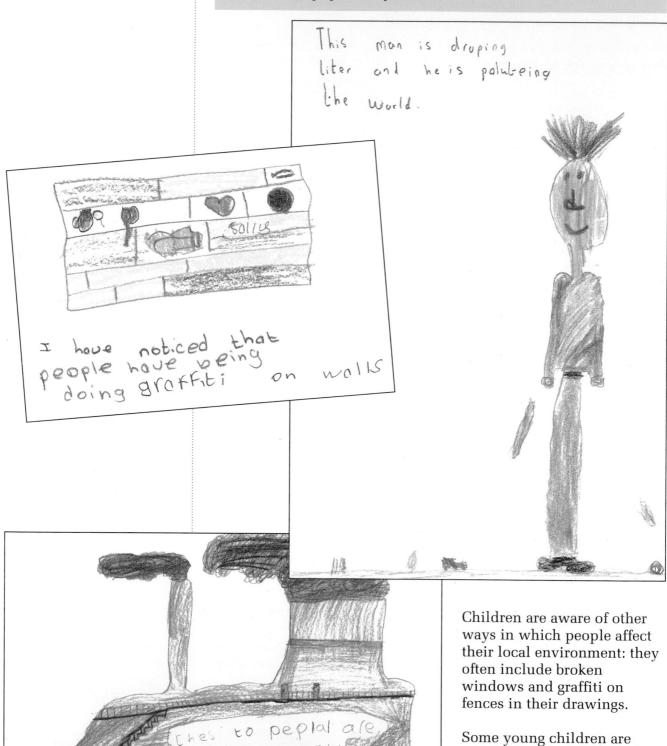

This man is druping liter and he is palubeing the World.

I have noticed that people have being doing graffiti on walls

thes to peplal are pluting The sky

Children are aware of other ways in which people affect their local environment: they often include broken windows and graffiti on fences in their drawings.

Some young children are aware of the ways in which the air and sea might be polluted.

Children do mention the positive effects that people have on the environment. They frequently say that homes could be redecorated, that graffiti could be painted over, or that new buildings could be built.

You plant more trees to keep the earth nice.

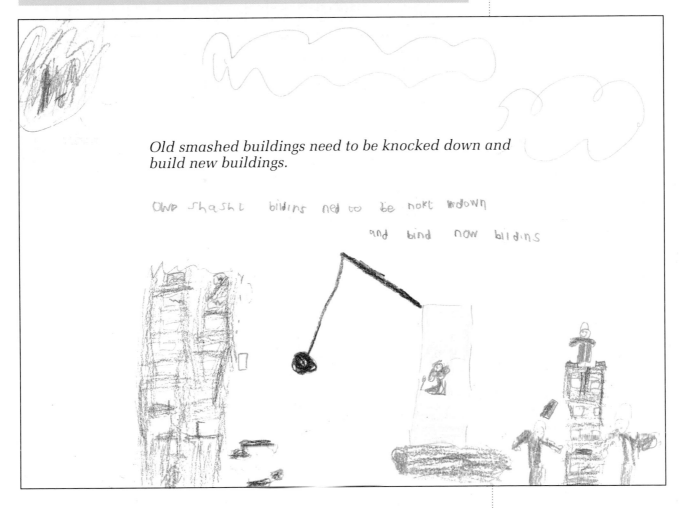

Old smashed buildings need to be knocked down and build new buildings.

Young children also mention how people affect one another. They point out that people fight, and suggest that improvements would encourage people to be nice to one another.

I would make it sunshine, so people will be kind to each other.

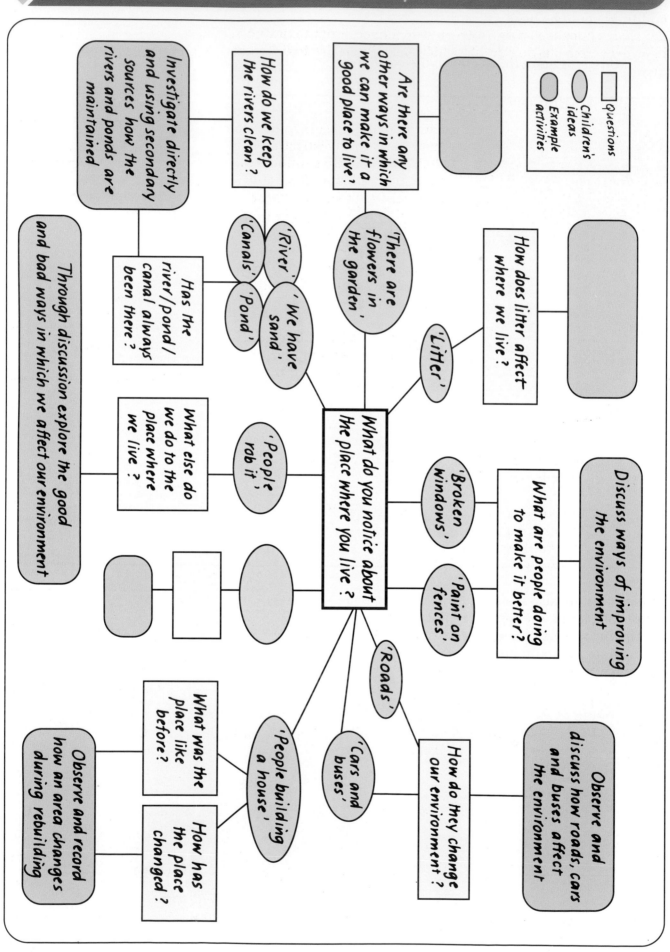

Key

Questions ▢
Children's ideas ⬭
Example activities ▭ (shaded)

What do you notice about the place where you live?

- 'There are flowers in the garden'
- 'River' / 'Canals' / 'Pond' / 'We have sand'
- 'Litter'
- 'People rob it'
- 'Broken windows'
- 'Paint on fences'
- 'Roads'
- 'People building a house'
- 'Cars and buses'

Are there any other ways in which we can make it a good place to live?

How do we keep the rivers clean?

Investigate directly and using secondary sources how the rivers and ponds are maintained

Has the river/pond/canal/canal always been there?

What else do we do to the place where we live?

Through discussion explore the good and bad ways in which we affect our environment

How does litter affect where we live?

What are people doing to make it better?

Discuss ways of improving the environment

How do they change our environment?

Observe and discuss how roads, cars and buses affect the environment

What was the place like before?

How has the place changed?

Observe and record how an area changes during rebuilding

Helping children to develop their ideas

The chart opposite shows how you can help children to develop their ideas from starting points which have given rise to different ideas.

1 Litter around the school

Children might begin to develop their ideas by investigating how their own activities influence their environment. You could take children to collect litter around the school and in the grounds. (Wear gloves or plastic bags on the hands when collecting litter or waste.) They could keep a diary of the litter they notice here.

Q *What kind of litter is it?*
Where do you find it?
Where do you find most litter?
How can you measure the amount of litter?

The investigations might help children to think of ways of discouraging people from dropping litter.

Q *How can you stop people from dropping litter?*
Is it left in some places because there are no bins?
Are the school bins in the best places?
What happens when the bins are full?

Children can make posters, collages or badges showing how litter affects the school environment. They might present a short play to other children to encourage them to put litter in the bin.

! Hygiene

AT 1 — Measuring Observing

AT 1 — Communicating

AT
1
Interpreting results and
findings

pb

Follow school or LEA rules
about supervision.
Check your school's policy on
visits

AT
1
Observing

Children may want to find out how successful their campaign is. Help them to identify patterns in their data and draw conclusions from their investigations.

Q *Are people dropping the same amount of litter? How do you know?*
Do the bins get too full?
Is the litter being dropped in different places or the same places as before?
Could we do anything else to stop the litter being dropped?

A first look at where things live encourages children to think about the origin of litter they might find in the local environment, and can be used to provide further discussions.

2 The [urban] environment

Take the children for a walk to look at the different ways in which human activity affects the local environment.

They could draw pictures of the things they notice, showing how the area might have been changed by people. Posing questions will increase children's awareness of how humans can change their environment.

Q *What are you walking on? Was this/were these made by people?*
What are the gratings at the side of the road for? Who put them there?
Are the streets light or dark at night?
How have people helped to make the streets light?
What do you notice about the fences?
Who has planted the flowers in the park?

Give the children an opportunity to discuss their observations, and to suggest reasons for the changes they notice.

Q *Has this place always looked like it does now?*
What made it change?

3 Changes in the air

The walk might give you a chance to guide children towards considering how human activity could affect the air and atmosphere.

 Can you see any smoke from the chimney?
How do you think the smoke was made?
Are there any other ways in which we put smoke into the air?

Children might make collages of magazine cuttings to show the ways in which people affect the atmosphere. Through discussion they might begin to consider some of the ways in which people have tried to reduce air pollution.

AT 1 — Communicating

4 Noise in the environment

Children might investigate the range of noises they can hear in different places during their walk, perhaps using a tape recorder.

AT 1 — Communicating
Observing

 Are there any noises
which are too loud?
What could people
do to make the world
a quieter place to live?

5 Looking at rivers and streams

It may be possible to draw children's attention to changes in streams, rivers or canals during the walk.

 What do you notice about the water?
Is there anything in the local streams which shouldn't be there?
Do you think the water will change or stay the same?
Do you think there will be any living things in the water?

Through class discussion children could think about some of the ways people try to protect the water we drink.

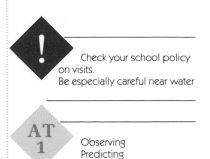
! Check your school policy on visits.
Be especially careful near water

AT 1 — Observing
Predicting

Q *Where does the water in our taps come from?*
Is it dirty or clean?
Who makes it clean?
What are reservoirs for?
How did people make the reservoirs?

AT 1   Communicating

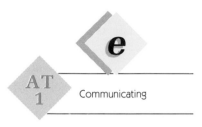

pb

pb

6   People and animals

Rhymes such as this might lead to consideration of how people affect animal life.

> *One, two, three four five,*
> *Once I caught a fish alive.*
> *Six, seven, eight nine ten,*
> *Then I let it go again.*

Q   *What happens when people catch fish?*
Why do people catch fish?

Children might find pictures, or make Plasticine models, of endangered animals – not only exotic species such as tigers, but local ones such as frogs. They should discuss with each other the possible reasons for the threat to these animals.

A first look at where things live encourages children to think about the effect of removing animals and plants from the seaside, and how hunting endangers elephants.

7   Improving the locality

Give children a picture of a landscape, such as the Dutch scene shown in *A first look at where things live*.

Ask questions that will encourage children to think about the ways in which people might have improved the environment.

Q   *Would you be able to live in the fields in this picture?*
Where in this picture would you like to live?

8   Setting up a wildlife area at school

It may be possible for children to take charge of a small piece of land in the school grounds.

t   A wildlife area will need careful planning and a lot of support from other people, including the school governors and possibly the LEA. Children should be encouraged to recognize that the area will need to be constantly maintained

!   Check the area for absence of dog mess, broken glass, and poisonous plants. Beware of buried pipes and cables

Can you describe what the place looks like now?
What do we want it to look like?
What kinds of animals do we want to attract?
What changes are necessary?
How will we make the changes?
Will we need to plan anything?
Could garden centres/shops/parents help us?

9 Changes in the locality

Children might be aware of local attempts to improve the environment which they could discuss. These could include clearing rubbish out of ponds or nettles and brambles from churchyards, making paths for walkers, rebuilding stone walls, traffic calming, cycle tracks, pedestrian areas.

They could use wall displays to show the improvements they would like to see in the area.

CHAPTER 3

Assessment

3.1 Introduction

You will have been assessing your children's ideas and skills by using the activities in this teachers' guide. This on-going, formative assessment is essentially part of teaching since what you find is immediately used in suggesting the next steps to help the children's progress. But this information can also be brought together and summarized for purposes of recording and reporting progress. This summary of performance has to be in terms of National Curriculum level descriptions at the end of the key stages, and some schools keep records in terms of levels at other times.

This chapter helps you summarize the information you have from children's work in terms of level descriptions. Examples of work relating to the theme of this guide are discussed and features which indicate activity at a certain level are pointed out to show what to look for in your pupils' work as evidence of achievement at one level or another. It is necessary, however, to look across the full range of work, and not judge from any single event or piece of work.

There are two sets of examples provided. The first is the assessment of skills in the context of the activities related to the concepts covered in this guide. The second deals with the development of these concepts.

3.2 Assessment of skills (AT1)

Things to look out for when pupils are investigating living things in their environments as indicating progress from level 1 to level 3:

Level 1: Making observations of the observable features of living things and of the places where they live; talking about and drawing them.

Level 2: Making suggestions as well as responding to others' suggestions about how to find things out or compare the conditions in which different plants and animals live. Using equipment in making observations, such as magnifying glasses, trowels and string to mark off small areas of habitats for study. Recording what they find and comparing it with what they expected.

Level 3: Saying what they expect to happen when something is changed or things are to be compared and suggesting ways of collecting information to test their predictions. Carrying out fair tests and fair comparisons, knowing why they are fair, and making measurements. Recording what they find in a variety of ways; noticing any patterns in it.

A Year 2 teacher planned to help the children understand some of the needs of living things by looking after and studying an animal or plant over a number of weeks. First they would visit the living things in their natural habitat to see what was there that they would need if they were to thrive in the classroom. They began with snails; later the teacher planned to have a wormery, to plant seeds and keep tadpoles, at the appropriate time of year.

After visiting a field nearby and finding snails, the children were asked what they had observed snails would need to live. Plastic boxes were set up with soil in the bottom and the snails were installed.

Vicky points out that the snails have to be in a box to stop them moving everywhere; she indicates the conditions that the snails need by explaining why there are holes in the box and that they are being given food and water. Although in terms of ideas this is at level 2, her work shows investigative skills at level 1 since it is essentially descriptive.

Vicky

The snails are in the box in case they escape. There are holes to give it fresh air. We are giving the snails food and wate

[Teacher annotation]

Lindsay's work shows detailed observation of a snail's movement and how it feels on her hand. She makes a suggestion that it moves slowly because of the weight of the shell, an idea based on her personal experience no doubt. Her work is at level 1, although with encouragement she might develop and try out ideas about how snails move and why they feel slimy, and so make progress towards level 2.

When a snail is on your hand it feels slimey and cold. It moves slowly because the shell is too heavy for it to move fast.

Lindsay

Stephen suggested that the snails were always in their shells because they were frightened of noise. His teacher asked him whether he could find out if this was the best reason. He said he would put them in a very quiet place and see if they would come out of their shells. He chose the spare classroom and asked to put them there and looked at them first thing next morning. He was not convinced, however, that it was really quiet enough and still expected them to be able to leave their shells. Stephen's response to his teacher's suggestion shows his investigative skills are progressing towards level 2.

Stephen's drawing shows how he tried to explain why the snails were in their shells. He carried out a simple investigation and obtained a result which he compared with what he expected. His work meets the requirement for level 2 and shows progress towards level 3.

The snails are frightened of noise. So that is why they are allways in their shells. We are feeding thme on cucumber and leaves.

Stephen

3.3 Assessment of children's understanding (Part of AT2)

In terms of work relating to living things in their environment, progress from level 1 to level 3 is indicated by:

Level 1: Awareness that there are different plants and animals in the environment.

Level 2: Awareness of the different conditions in local environments and that these affect the living things found there.

Level 3: Identifying ways in which animals and plants familiar to them are suited to their habitats.

The drawings of Juliet and Dawn (shown opposite) show an awareness of a number of different living things. In Juliet's drawing there is an indication for only some of the living things of where they are found: some of the plants are in soil, the snail is shown on the ground and the cat in the house. These give little evidence of awareness of the conditions in which each lives and thus the work is at level 1.

Juliet

Dawn's drawing illustrates places where the living things might be found and shows awareness that each has a different habitat. Discussion about how the conditions in different environments might affect the things there would help to confirm her work at level 2.

Dawn

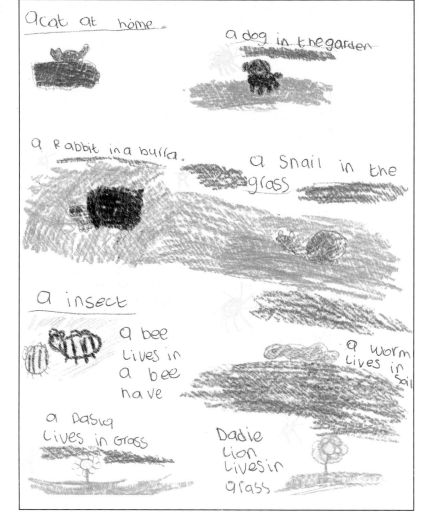

Kate discussed her drawings of the cactus and spider plant with her teacher. She is beginning to generalize about what 'all plants need' but knows that some need more water than others. The teacher might probe about the places in which these two plants are found naturally in order to decide whether Kate recognized a relationship between the different needs of the plants and the conditions in the habitats. This would help to decide whether Kate's work has reached level 3.

Kate:	*The spider plant needs water. The cactus needs a little bit of water. All plants need soil and sun. The spider plant needs sun.*
Teacher:	*Why does the spider plant need sun?*
Kate:	*The sun keeps it healthy. If it has no sun it won't grow.*

Kate

Index